# DARK AS A
# HAZEL EYE

## COFFEE & CHOCOLATE POEMS

## THE RAGGED SKY POETRY SERIES

# DARK AS A HAZEL EYE

## COFFEE & CHOCOLATE POEMS

**EDITED BY ELLEN FOOS, VASILIKI KATSAROU AND LYNNE SHAPIRO**

Ragged Sky Press
Princeton, New Jersey

Published by Ragged Sky Press

P.O. Box 312, Annandale, NJ 08801

www.raggedsky.com

Library of Congress Control Number: 2015914081

ISBN: 978-1-933974-18-7

A list of acknowledgments appears in the back of this book.

Designed by Diane Thibault, Greene Street Creative

This book is composed in Bembo and Verlag

Manufactured in the United States of America

First Edition

A cup of coffee—real coffee—home-browned, home ground, home made, that comes to you dark as a hazel-eye, but changes to a golden bronze as you temper it with cream that never cheated, but was real cream from its birth, thick, tenderly yellow, perfectly sweet, neither lumpy nor frothing on the Java: such a cup of coffee is a match for twenty blue devils and will exorcise them all.

—Henry Ward Beecher

# CONTENTS

## Bitter

## Ritual

## Afterlife

## INTRODUCTION

Of the three basic necessities of life, food seems to me the most sensuous.
Although coffee and chocolate are not high on the list for survival, they do com
up often in poetry. Coffee typically signifies the bitter and chocolate the sweet.
Both of them have enough associations to fill a psychiatrist's waiting room.
There is loss of innocence and sin. Aptly-named poet Coco Owen calls truffles
"pussy-tongued."

The poets who have contributed to this volume do not always follow the
standard assumptions. They make us think twice about death and desire. As
Catherine Barnett asks, "What do they put in this coffee? Men?" We get stories
shared over coffee and chocolate eaten in hiding. We want our cravings satisfied
in very particular ways. Christopher Bullard wants his coffee "so black I expecte
to see stars in it."

Ritual and addiction are close companions in these poems. They can be treated
lightly or with immense seriousness. Do poets turn to coffee or chocolate for
lack of better totems? Michael Palmer asks a woman he meets to drink from his
"cup's perfect emptiness." I invite readers to see if this anthology takes them
back to childhood, or to a raunchy roadhouse, or perhaps tucks them in at nigh
Hopefully not wired up on caffeine.

Ellen Foc

I could tell the story of my life through coffee. From the first coffee I ever
tasted at 14 in the church basement at an American Friends Service meeting in
Andover, Massachusetts, to the college coffee dates at Café Pamplona or Café
Algiers, or Coffee Connection in Cambridge.... I followed the river of coffee
and it led me to the pleasures of lingering, to stolen glances, to connoisseurship
and to poetry and art.

In my 20s, I picked up and moved to a center of coffee culture: Paris. I lived
near the Sorbonne, and slipped into Parisian urban life by spending time in
storied cafés all over the Left Bank. I discovered new favorites—
café crème in the morning, and a noisette (hazelnut) anytime later on.

When in Greece, I savored the thimbleful of thick bitter coffee that was misguidedly called "Turkish." A single shot or a double, with sugar measured out as *sketo, metrio* or *glyko* (plain, medium sweet, sweet). A single metrio was my drink of choice, though an icy cold coffee frappé is always a good choice for a hot afternoon. Since Greece adopted the euro, coffee spots have gotten more expensive, and the new coffee craze in Greece is for the Italian version of the Greek frappé, now called the *freddo* (cappuccino).

But small Greek cups were good not just for caffeination, but for divination. In the years after college and before I wed, I dared to dabble in the art of reading the dregs of Greek coffee. I'd flip a cup over into its saucer and peer inside. A miniature landscape invariably presented itself inside a white ceramic cone. It forecast a future, a river, a peninsula. Whatever it was that I told friends or my future mother-in-law, I was convincing. My brief career as a fortune-teller was successful.

The only time I stopped drinking coffee was during the nine months I was pregnant with my son. I quit cold turkey because I knew little sips would do me in, and I avoided cafés. I felt content in my conviction that my progeny would have the best possible beginning without a caffeine-addled little brain. But during his toddler years, I was back in tight with my favorite elixir. My Greek mother now called me "kafóbriko"—named after the long-handled beaten copper Greek briki coffee pot. I was only satisfied with a fruity, smoky brew. Nothing watered down or percolated.

I have friends who are tea drinkers but, truth be told, I don't altogether trust them and their overly subtle palates. For me, tea is hot water with a slight flavoring added.

I find it hard to imagine a long stretch of writing without access to some good coffee. I've been known to travel to relatives or to writing workshops with my Italian screwtop espresso maker, and my Melitta filter, just in case.

My coffee-colored dachshund Melville is also a coffee-lover like me. Each morning he waits eagerly for me to bring my mug to the couch or armchair so that he can sit on my lap while I sip. I have seen him lap up espresso when given the opportunity, but he also enjoys simply imbibing the coffee-scented air wafting from my cup. I've observed him chomping on his coffee-steeped cone of air. Beware, anyone who tries to move him from such existential treats!

It is a great pleasure to sample the varied work of so many fine poets on the subjects of coffee and chocolate. I hope you will smile with recognition at all the places both physical and metaphysical that coffee can take us.

Vasiliki Katsarou

When it comes to chocolate, the miracle of transforming a bitter, impenetrable pod into something you can eat is an argument for how cultured the ancients were. And I can think of no other tree with fruit that grows from the trunk. Years ago, I even wrote an essay about my fervent desire to spend the night beneath the cocoa tree in the Enid A. Haupt Conservatory of the New York Botanical Garden in the Bronx, in the hopes of winning just this dreamy prize. It remains on my bucket list.

I remember when I opened the package containing a cocoa pod that I purchased on eBay many years ago, an undercurrent of chocolate filled the room. I kept it on my desk where the scent inspired me each time I sat down to write. Every year now, I'm invited into the kindergarten classes at the school where I work to talk about the curious pod. Pollination and reproduction, the first hints of a sex talk—and yet no one even blinks. I print out photos of trees, cocoa pods, and images of chocolate production—but what's most surprising to the children is that there are chocolate *flowers*. (Of course there are…but still!)

My own interest in chocolate goes back to my passion in elementary school for anything Mayan and Aztec. At a recent exhibition of Mayan chocolate vessels at Princeton University, I felt the same frisson I felt so many years ago. Vasiliki, co-editor of this anthology, joined me there. As a potter, she found the vessels surprisingly ordinary in shape. For me they were blank pages upon which hieroglyphic stories about power and politics were preserved. Painted for the Mayan court, they both commemorate the occasions where chocolate was served and preserve an ancient relationship between image and word.

On my first day of Spanish class in junior high school, I was introduced to a Mexican song, which we sang as we rubbed our palms together, pretending to stir hot chocolate *(champurrado)* with a *molinillo* (a whisk) into a froth: *Bate, bate, chocolate / Tu nariz de cacahuate / Uno, dos, tres: CHO! / Uno, dos, tres: CO! / Uno, dos, tres: LA! / Uno, dos, tres: TE! / Chocolate, chocolate! / Bate, bate, chocolate.* As I spoke those exotic words (I was 12) something indescribable happened in my mouth and I fell in love with language. I still love words like chocolatl and, in the Aztec's Nahuatl language, *xocoatl* or *cacahuatl* (which means "bitter water"). The Nahuatl word, cacao (source of the English word, *cocoa*) refers to the bean itself. The plant's botanical name, *Theobroma cacao* (which means "food of the gods") is delightful to say.

I purchased my own *molinillo* on Olvera Street during one of my last visits to Los Angeles, my childhood home. Though inexpensive, it is handmade using a wood lathe, and is remarkably beautiful to me. On that last trip, I also visited the Grand Central Market to purchase mole sauce. There, a woman sells several kinds of homemade moles. No need for refrigeration here—the mole is made of ground spices, chiles, and chocolate. There's nowhere I have found on the East Coast where I can purchase freshly made, unpackaged mole. (Please contact me if you know otherwise.)

You may notice, my personal connection to chocolate has more to do with culture and less to do with tasting chocolate. But I would like to close with a more personal memory of a family ritual. My mother would make a pot of Droste cocoa and pour it into espresso cups for the two of us to drink. This was always a special time for us. It was before she remarried, and something only we shared. The set was handed down to me so that I could share the same tradition with my son.

May I suggest, then, before peeling open the poems to come, that you spend some time thinking about your own personal connections to chocolate and coffee.

Lynne Shapiro

# BUZZ

Coffee is a match for twenty bue devils.

—Henry Ward Beecher

Elaine Equi
## CIAO BELLA CHOCOLATE SORBET

has a dense
chewy

water to chocolate
ratio

as if a whole
devil's food cake

were dissolved
in each scoop.

Delivers Elvis-like
indulgence

for only 120 calories.
By the last spoonful,

your whole nervous system
and aura

will be permeated
by the ancient Mayan God.

You will see
through the eyes of Chocolate.

Therese Sellers
# COFFEE HAIKU

1.

Coffee, dark and strong
Or muddy and prophetic
Or dressed like a monk.

2.

A cappuccino
You stirred the foam with a spoon
Cyprian goddess.

3.

At midnight my son
Brought me a cup of coffee
Don't sleep, I need you.

4.

Caution contents hot
I read on my coffee lid
And sipped sweet danger.

5.

Like a lioness
Dragging her kill, I drag my
Coffee back to bed.

Carol Buckley
## COFFEE BLISS


There is a weight
to coffee other liquids do not have
—soup too meaty, tea too light.
Coffee weighs your thoughts and brings
them down to earth: culinary cousin
to a yellow, lined legal pad,
astringent key to one's direction.
Coffee can spin you like a top, like
Sufi monks who first tasted
the burnt bliss of the dark brew,
set down their cups and twirled
into a mystic world. Digging
deeper with each turn,
connecting earth
and holy
sky

Elizabeth Danson
## ENTICED

With coffee, it's the sideshow—the surroundings
that conjure a world long gone, or poked into
dusty corners of back streets and bazaars. It's
the equipment of leisure, of passionate discourse,
of ceremony: the copper pot with its long handle,
tiny cups on the engraved tray that becomes a table.
The dark liquid pour, the harsh hit to the palate,
the way the contents of the cup imitate a pond—
clear on top, deepening to sediment at the bottom,
and the decision about just how far down to go.

Katrin Talbot
**MY FIRST TURK**

Dark booth,
Berkeley, 1981.
Why not? I thought.
It's time, after all the
gallons of college coffee
I had imbibed in that handmade
Mexican mug the size of Kansas,
fueling my thesis all-nighters

The tiny gilded cup arrived with a
casual Mediterranean flick of the wrist
and I gazed into the foam of a caramel ocean

What was needed before a race, before
a song, a deep inhale, and then I fell
slowly into the sweet vessel, back
into the Black Sea's embrace,
and, after all that, a flip of
the cup for me to fall out
into a fortunetelling of
my simple destiny:
more dark eyes
and another
*Türk kahvesi*

Please.

Rosemary Wright
## WHAT YOU NEED


When you wake up in the morning,
your head a deck of cards scattered on the floor,
you need coffee.

You need fragrant coffee.
So fragrant you float on scent,
ancient and ethereal,
frankincense from Babylonian rites.
Earthy too,
the smell of mud on a sunny day in early spring.

You need strong coffee.
Strong like a body builder,
a squad of Marines fresh from boot camp.
Strong like the mother
lifting a car to free her child.

You need hot coffee.
Not too hot like Icelandic lava.
You need coffee hot like Sean Connery in *Thunderball*
or Lena Horne singing "The Man I Love."

You need black coffee.
Black like tar from prehistoric pits
when mastodons still roamed.
Black like shadows cast by trees
in moonlight on a mountaintop at midnight.

You need rich coffee.
Smooth and rich,
Bavarian vanilla cream pie.

You need bitter coffee.
Not bitter like tears you shed
for the Valentine that never came.
No, not that bitter.
You need coffee bitter like a dab of truth
which hurts for a moment then sets you free.

You need coffee now.
Inhale. Exhale. Sip.
Feel fireflies buzzing through your veins,
the sun rising over Kilimanjaro,
the earth spinning.

Joan Fishbein
**MOUTHFUL**


a slice
now and then
filled with substances
that sweeten your mood
feed your brain
speed your heart
perhaps created
by a baker
whose semantic skill
rivaled his recipe
he might have been
Marie Antoinette's
political kin
paying lip service
to the perfect end
of any meal
where what's at stake
is  texture  desire  taste
Death By Chocolate
cake which poses
the biting question
is there a better way to go

Carlos Hernández-Peña
## BITTER SWEET


Yesterday
        I thought I lost you—
between chocolate I didn't bake
and poems I didn't write
                        except
you stepped out of this reverie
without doors


Today    I caught a glimpse
of your figure in black attire—
blood surged out of rhythm
I mumbled and drowned words


This stolen image of you
                      reminded me
Indeed
        you still exist
                inside the sixth day
of the lunar fortnight
                    and outside
            a dark chocolate fantasy

Ruth Zamoyta
## AT THE LAKE HOUSE


The stars deserve the night and so the embers
whose glow cannot stir this black lake
like the quiet rings of the loon.
Firelight flicks on the pages of my book,
laid down on my lap as I pause for coffee
and turn toward the call of the wolf.

Calls are meant and so the wolf's,
in spite of my scent and the crackling embers
which warm my feet as my belly fills with coffee.
The faithful lapping of the lake
keeps beat with the turning pages of my book
for the lonesome call of the loon.

Bass and trout, clam and minnow, heron, loon,
thrush and osprey, deer, fox, wolf—
make the lake a larger stage than any book
for the playing out of thought in shifting embers,
and the shiver of moonlight upon the lake
which I watch for signs with my mug of coffee.

He said he was going for a beer, and left me with a mug of coffee—
alone on this island ignored by the loon
and the million blinded creatures of the lake.
Another howl, and I guess that wolves
can swim, and wonder if I should throw a log on those embers.
I decide he doesn't care, and open my book.

There is no meaning in nature, as there is in my book—
no theme in the wind nor sign in the vapors of coffee;
no point to the rustle of boughs; no message in the embers;
no higher purpose in the path of the loon.
No one ordained the closeness of the wolf
but the wolf, as he approaches the lake.

The stars depart the night and so the lake,
mute but I know it's there. I touch my book,
inscrutable in the dying fire. The wolf
draws near. I shiver, sip my coffee,
and find it cold. I cannot hear the loon.
The cool of the night has vanquished all the embers.

I rise and turn from the lake, and spill out the coffee,
Recalling less the book than the laugh of the loon,
The cry of the wolf, and the lapse of the last ember.

# CRAVING

It was like having a box of chocolates shut in the bedroom drawer. Until the box was empty it occupied the mind too much.
—Graham Greene, *The Heart of the Matter*

Mary Cheever
# THE NEED FOR CHOCOLATE

The need for chocolate or other sweets,
like liquor for some, drugs
or one sole lover more than any other—shrug
the question that has no answer: what makes one
person need another this way? Until the way is gone—
sweet mouthing and melting chocolate,
                                   whatever you crave
as comfort or just desert, but should not have
because it rots the teeth or strains the heart,
learn to do without.
                    You have plenty of bread,
lockers of well hung meat,
loads of greens and green perfect fruits
trucked in from distant states.
Your need for chocolate is all in your head.
                              You think you want it.
You're better off without it. Break the habit.

Catherine Barnett
## ACTS OF MIND

What's funny about this place
is us regulars coming in with our different
accoutrements, mine usually the little void
of space I call honey, days
I can barely get through I'm laughing so hard,
see? In the back a woman squeezes oranges,
someone presses the fresh white bread
into communion wafers or party favors.
In the window the chickens rotate blissfully,
questioning nothing—
Sometimes I flirt with the cashier, just improvising,
the way birds land all in a hurry on the streetlamp across the street,
which stays warm even on cold nights.
Guillaume says humor is sadness
and he's awfully pretty.
What do they put in this coffee? Men?
No wonder I get a little high. Remember
when we didn't have sex on the Ferris wheel,
oh that was a blast,
high, high above the Tuileries!

Amy Miller
## MR. COFFEE


I dreamt you out of the pot for hours,
wandered down the Cost Plus counter,
choosing your brown body, your paper wrap

smelling of smoke and cocoa.
You climbed inside me,
drove me fast and breathless

through the scaffolding of day.
How you whispered of the *lovely*,
then dropped me on a street

ten miles from home
with an uphill walk.
Later you slapped me, kept me up

counting the sins of my future,
dragged me out of bed again
for the capillaries of your tongue.

How I finally could not see
past the beads you shook so hard,
heard my own ears shouting.

How you never really
loved me. How you flashed
a hundred girls a morning

in the bright café,
their fingers sliding through your loop
and holding their lips to yours.

Coco Owen
# HOT-TODDY TRUFFLE


These pussy-tongued, chocolate *langues de chat*
Are the bon-bons I whipped up while well-liquored.
I do lay it on thick, which can put off some.
But if you grew up on the Hershey's kisses

& Cool-Whip-topped Jell-O which passed
For poetic fare where I grew up eating,
So would you. I make these poetic
Edibles to love-substitute:

Here—Try this hot-toddy truffle. Or this
Chocolate-martini bite which gives more bang
Than any Godiva's tired, gold-foiled strip-tease.
Let this truffle tempt you to just desserts.

Theodore Eisenberg
## BITCH CHOCOLATE

I love your layered
night, the hard nut
of your freedom.
I swim within a vat
of your beginnings,
great dismal swamp.
Bitterns wade long-legged,
their beaks accuse the mire.
I unwrap and eat you;
the drizzle of your taste
stains my lips with
blood of black cherry

Dannie Abse
## CHOCOLATE BOX

Late neglected November, Leporello,
and more back-garden rosy-red apples
decorated the tree than countable leaves
when she, through the window,
saw a blue tit on a bough.

Sighed: "What an unbelievable pretty picture,
an old-fashioned chocolate-box."

Later, surprised, thinking of unpicked apples,
of course I tasted her red pretty mouth.

Later still, at twilight, the unwrapping.
Her falling black dress rustling
like chocolate-paper;

and the whole delicious
old-fashioned, Rubens-beautiful
box open. Offered and taken: truffle,
cherry liqueur, marzipan, Turkish Delight.

Maxine Susman
## A TASTING GAME


We play Truffles only once or twice a year.
I play it with my husband, played it with my children
when they were small—a game for kids or lovers.

Start with a little white box of assorted miracles
from Birnn's, the neighborhood candy factory
whose chocolates rival the best from Belgium.

If you go first, choose one. Memory
will lead you, or impulse, or careful deliberation,
or just close your eyes and lift one out

and nibble on its edge. A tiny bite, merely
enough to taste its flavor on your tongue.
Do you remember this, or is it new?

Lemon champagne mint hazelnut raspberry,
amaretto, dulce de leche, orange, key lime,
sometimes blueberry, sometimes maple.

Milk chocolate. Dark chocolate. Don't lick.
Then pass the truffle to the person nearest you
who takes a nibble, lingers, savors, passes it on

to who's next. Everybody takes a taste and then
whoever likes it most will eat what's left.
Each person has a turn to choose, a turn to finish.

Truffles will teach you concentration. Foreplay.
That you and someone else can want the same thing,
but rarely want it equally. That many flavors beckon:

if you forfeit one, another tastes delicious too.
That triumphs and concessions stay sweet when small.
How to make something last that isn't meant to last.

Lois Marie Harrod
# THE CIRCUS OF MOANS

That old electric coffeepot used to come
        every morning in a circus of moans–

ah, we sighed, taking the first sip, love–
        the reliable start to any story.

Later we sagged like teachers escaping
        to relieving rooms, groaning on cue.

Respite, we begged, a break from the clowns,
        stall beyond the jitter juice.

And yet we knew almost everything worth making
        took mud of one sort or other.

Whimpers deep in the snow day, children asleep,
        we looked up as flakes brewed.

Silent sigh of swan feathers the day that golfer
        found a mask on the course.

Look, he said, holding it by the hair, then
        dropped the thing, seeing what it was.

Love comes like that too, head-float down Stony Brook
        not far from where we were simpering.

She was a woman from Brooklyn where poets
        jolt joe among the ailanthus.

No cover-ups since that blizzard, nothing to quell
          the train rumbling to a snore.

Would you write if every word could be
          effaced like graffiti on a coal car?

This is a kind of composition too,
          you cupping the pillow beside me.

We drank so much coffee then,
          pots and pots of perk.

We were so wired—
          lovers grinding down the murk.

# BLISS

How sweet coffee tastes,
more delicious than a thousand kisses

—J. S. Bach, "Coffee Cantata"

Adrianne Kalfopoulou
# I MARVEL

at how I smile, make coffee
in the morning, spread the wet grounds, smell
the black liquid drip, enjoy the heat as I sit
in the quietly breaking day.
I marvel that I am able to think of
a month from now, plan a vacation, realize
the day will have me teach, drive to school
and back, pause at a fruit stand, hold
the pomegranate's shape, the garlic's curved
clove nape. I'm amazed I wash
the soap from my face, dry my skin, feel
its tightness with delight, see everything
transformed into beloved light as though I've found
my best friend's hand in blind night.

Jody Struve
## THE BEGINNING OF MY NAME


1.

my mother closed her eyes
and whispered names until
she felt dirt falling
from a hand
fresh dirt
falling from a strong hand
fingers spread
         open
and when she whispered once more
the calloused hand plunged again
into the soft earth of a sun filled field.


2.

I sit in the small world coffee shop and think
each shout for a cup of "joe"
is the beginning of my name.
the first syllable of love.
it has nothing to do with lonely.
it is not because my need for touch has moved
as deep as the sweet caress of the inner ear.
it is because of the steady rhythm
that I look up
turn my head each time to see
who is calling,
who might have come.

BJ Ward
# AUBADE

I love how this morning the world spills
around my breakfast plate, the newspaper opened beneath it—
Kosovo's rebuilding next to my toast
as my mug rests atop the list of celebrity birthdays.
Today's morning is large enough for Alfred Hitchcock and Don Ho
to have the same birthday, both residents now
on the continent of my kitchen table. The coffee machine
warbles its symphony of frogs and radiators
as if to sing of the arrival of the coffee itself.
The fried eggs start applauding.
Before I can stand, Victoria and her green eyes
float into the room and dock on the shores
of my table's new democracy, pouring me a cup.
And I want to be as precise with my joy today
as all those poets are with their suffering.
I want to tell you how on August 13th I was happy
even as the world surrounded my breakfast.
Now I see Fidel Castro and Danny Bonaduce share
this birthday also and they will forever be linked in my mind
with Hitchcock and Don Ho, and that's all right,
because this was the day the coffee and the light and
Victoria's sculptured neckline were pieces of my life breaking
open, and how they conspired to make the world

once more bearable again and again and again.

Dorothea Grossman
## I ALLOW MYSELF

I allow myself
the luxury of breakfast
(I am no nun, for Christ's sake).
Charmed as I am
by the sputter of bacon,
and the eye-opening properties
of eggs,
it's the coffee
that's really sacramental.
In the old days,
I spread fires and floods and pestilence
on my toast.
Nowadays, I'm more selective,
I only read my horoscope
by the quiet glow of the marmalade.

Dean Kostos
## TASTE

*All tastes have hidden rooms / Within the Tongue.*
                    —Thomas Traherne


It's Sunday, or is it sundae? I'm always hungry
          for sweets, especially chocolate.
                    A cocoa-colored colt appears.

I ride it to the creamy language
          of yesterday, pass
                    steppes of Central Asia, arrive

in Russia—time zone: tomorrow.
          As the colt caracoles,
                    then slows, I'm aware of taste

draining from my palate.
          I bend down, search
                    for it in the tongues of my shoes,

not roan or roam,
          but cordovan—no matter,
                    any brown reminds me of chocolate

& the tingling loss
          on my wandering tongue.
                    The road curves & tapers.

Will it lead where gestation
          has gone? A pigeon the color
                    of Chekhov's hair

lands on a branch to sip dew.
        "Have you seen my sense of taste?"
            I ask. The bird wings

into a cherry orchard. Could my sense
        be there? Clusters, voluptuous & crimson.
            Where else would taste take cover?

I stomp through the field of stumps—
        each one like Philomela's
            tongue. The bird alights

again. Which tree?
        I listen to the *langue* of my going,
            the voice of not knowing my path

& come upon a Fabergé tree. Pressing
        on its trunk, I'm ushered
            through a trapdoor, no one inside.

Padding into room after upholstered
        room, I reach a mahogany throne.
            Not wood—chocolate. I plunge

into its cushion & from its armrest,
        break off the carving of a pigeon
            that flutters into my mouth—Mmm…

# BITTER

Our culture runs on coffee and gasoline, the first often

tasting like the second.

—Edward Abbey, *Down the River*

Richard Brautigan
## XEROX CANDY BAR

Ah,

you're just a copy

of all the candy bars

I've ever eaten.

Ishmael von Heidrick-Barnes
## AIRLIFT

for Lt. Gail "Hal" Halvorson


Berlin's children
bombed
barefoot

Famished city of facades
cratered eyes sunk in rubble

Mounds of brick
beneath a bridge of C-47 cargo planes
landing
bellies swollen with coal
for winter's cold front

Blocks of human beings
divided into sectors
corridors corroded
blockaded

Caught
between the Russian Bear
and the Candy Bombers

Full flaps
nose diving over stacks
wings waving handkerchiefs of Hershey Bars
gum dropping parachutes through
iron curtain sky

Bonbons away
over tree stripped tear gardens

The battle for spoils of war
won with chocolates

Chris Bullard
## A CUP OF JOE

When I ordered coffee from the Greek diner the counterman asked
if I wanted my coffee "regular." "Sure," I said, thinking "regular"
meant "plain," that is, coffee as it is naturally, black and strong. So,
when my coffee came back the light brown color of fallen leaves
and reeking of sweetness, I refused to pay. This led to an argument
with the counterman and then with the owner that was conducted
on my side in perfect English and on their side in a mixture of Greek
and heavily accented English that made it impossible for me to
convince them that their misuse of the word "regular" was wrong and
misleading and stupid. This is what got me sent back to the VA to see
my shrink of record, Dr. Kory, who brewed me some excellent Arabic
coffee that was so strong that it tasted like a blow to the head. "Think
of this coffee, Sergeant," Dr. Kory said, "it's a mixture. Roasted beans
are ground up and brewed with water. Simple enough, but the way I
make it may not be the way someone else makes it. People make it a
million different ways. Coffee means more than one thing." "Yeah,"
I thought, "and the glass is really half full." I know what "regular"
coffee is. I know what words mean. Some people think "right" and
"wrong" are just words, but I know the difference. I remember all
those brown bodies we left lying beside the road rotting with their
sickly sweet odor. It's only because I know that what we did was right
that I can put them from my mind. So, I smiled and pretended I was
listening. After they let me out, I went home and brewed myself
some coffee. I poured it into my Airborne mug and watched the steam
rising from the liquid that was as black as the nights back in the
Middle East. It was so black I almost expected to see the stars in it.

R. G. Evans
# IN THE CAFÉ AT THE END OF THE WORLD


The surface of my latte trembles
as if it wants to scream

*Something terrible is coming*
and of course it is.

That Richtering underfoot is the wrecking ball
smashing one more childhood into dust,

it's the emanations from an IED someone's favorite
uncle just triggered by the side of the road,

it's the wall of water rushing toward the sunken city
where not even dogs or chickens are safe up on the roofs,

it's the bombast of thunder that roars in the dark, saying
*Fear? Yes, fear, the next one will be closer still,*

it's the footsteps of the giant father in your dreams
burst from your unconscious and coming down the hall.

We huddle under tables for two,
pray to the gods of fair trade,

make our last confessions to baristas
too lost in the ecstasy of macchiato

to absolve even themselves.
I hold my paper cup like a chalice,

begging its runic ripples to help me understand,
but the best it can do is preach in Portuguese

about what happens when the mountain
finally decides to come down.

Hayden Saunier
## TABLE


Here we heard the story of how we almost never were.
We were eating chicken, rice and butter beans.

Father was flying, both wings dead with ice
above the tidal marshes, no solid ground

inside the magic circle of his calculations,
for him, the center point, to land,

so we were falling too. We felt ourselves

begin to disappear, the plates to tremble, milk
to slosh inside our cups, we banked

hard left and watched the biscuit basket
sliding past the fruit bowl, watched our sticky

rice-flecked hands steam prints that vanished
from the tabletop, we stalled and spiraled

down into the center of his cautionary tale—

below us, turbulence; legs twisting, kicking,
brothers crying, sisters trying not to pee—

until at last he dove toward the smokestacks
of a rendering plant, where we are lifted

by the heat of horses' hooves and hides, ice
melting off, wings clear, we wing it home,

our lives intact, our lesson learned,

our landing smooth as the imperturbable surface
of a Mother's chocolate silk pie.

Vasiliki Katsarou
## CHOCOLATE CREDIT CARD


In a deep blue wrapper
embossed with a seal and a cross
this chocolate is dark and labeled
"medicinal"

no frills, thin, Greek and *sweet enough*
though later Hershey bars
would be more welcome

from Diomedes, my great uncle,
abstemious widower who lived on
near textile mills downtown,

prayed twice a day
at Transfiguration Church with Father John,
nephew of his late wife, gone

too young
whose name I bear,
my middle one, *Anneta.*

Just the sight of my brother and me
was a joy, no longer another old bachelor,
my immigrant father was finally settled,

with a young wife from the village
and that earned us one Hershey Bar each.

This was our currency, then,
and sugar our denomination.

O for all these lost sources of sweetness
I too depend on you,
dark tablet

in your plastic sleeve, in a purse
or in my room,
held in reserve

for when its application to the tongue
is a salve to heal
a wound too obscure, too alchemical

to name.

# RITUAL

A poem is a café. (Restoration.)

—Wallace Stevens, from "Adagia"

Jennifer Arin
## XOCOLATL


Aztec kings and lords imbibed *xocolatl,*
a ground-cocoa-bean-and-chili beverage
which, in that cacao-tippling tongue, Náhuatl,
meant *bitter* (xococ) *water* (atl), a honeyed privilege

certainly no average
Aztec could earn.  In those days,
cacao beans had quite the leverage—
say, in the Tlatelolco marketplace

where, for 100 beans, nobles could pay
to have their burdens toted by a *Mexica* porter,
and for 3,000 beans, they could buy a slave
or wife. We've learned to sweeten that bitter order;

*Tatlí!* We drink! Let none of us be bitten
by hunger, or split by thirst. *Icuilotoc:* It is written.

James Richardson
## EMERGENCY MEASURES


I take Saturday's unpopulated trains,
sitting at uncontagious distances,
change at junctions of low body count, in off hours,
and on national holidays especially, shun stadia
and other zones of efficient kill ratio,
since there is no safety anymore in numbers.

I wear the dull colors of nesting birds,
invest modestly in diverse futures,
views and moods undiscovered by tourists,
buy nothing I can't carry or would need to sell,
and since I must rest, maintain at several addresses
hardened electronics and three months of water.

And it is thus I favor this unspecific café,
choose the bitterest roast, and only the first sip
of your story, sweet but so long, and poignantly limited
by appointments neither of us can be late for, and why now
I will swim through the crowd to the place it is flowing away from,
my concerned look and *Excuse me excuse me* suggesting
I am hurrying back for my umbrella or glasses
or some thrilling truth they have all completely missed.

Susan Cohen
# REPORTORIAL

I met them young and frightened.
It was San Francisco in the '80s.
In the Castro, the last bitter Irish bar
held out against their gayness,
and boys who had survived
a father's belt, boots to the ribs,
bottles smashed against their skulls,
showed a different kind of bruising
smacked purple by cancer
that spoiled their handsome faces.
Some seemed baffled
by the microbes in their brains.
I came to them as a reporter,
and they'd offer up their stories
with a cup of coffee I would sip
to show them their saliva did
not scare me. I remember one—
his army jacket hung on a frame
that had carried twice the weight.
Now he was a hanger for his coat.
We talked in a cafeteria, and then
he stood and hugged me too hard
for a stranger. He was a tall man
in his twenties who needed me

to know he was not a ghost yet, and
clung as if I were the raft to save him.
Or as if...and I'm still sorry, sorry
I imagined, face pressed against
rough cloth and the sharpness
of his shoulder, he almost hoped
to give me his disease. A reason
to remember how he felt.

Kiki Petrosino
# MUSTANG BAGEL

Even at my favorite coffeeshop downtown, Redford
is a hard man to feed. This morning, he picks
at his Grilled Asiago Mastercrust with a slow, disdainful frown.
*Could they spare the fromage on this so-called "treat?"*
He takes a sip of hazelnut coffee, then winces delicately
into the neck of his sweater vest. I bite powerfully
through my Cinnamon Frenchroll: *Well, if you really don't think
you got enough—"fromage"—you should just go back up there
& tell the girl.* I start on Redford's coffee while he looks glumly
at the metal napkin dispenser. Just then, the electric chime
above the door sounds. A man sweeps in & rests
his guitar case on one of the slim café chairs.
His dark hair is arranged in a series of perpetually
breaking wavefronts. A small muscle jumps in his jaw
as he orders a Cinnamon Frenchroll, toasted, with cream cheese.
I lean forward, jabbing Redford with my plastic coffee wand.
*Check out that guy over there* I say. *Intense.*
Redford shrugs. *I think he's Irish* I say, watching the man bite
into his bagel. The instrument case hovers on the chair edge.
He could have a guitar in there, or else—a sword from the Crusades.
I press my tongue into the square-shaped hole in the lid
of my coffee cup. *Listen* Redford says. *If we're going to be together
you have to take this.* He pushes a small velvet box across the table.
*What are you doing?* I ask, but Redford doesn't answer.
He just looks down at the table, one hand pressed
to each of his temples. In the box is a square of chocolate
like the top of a signet ring, smooth, but edged

in something bright. *It's smoked salt from Wales,* Redford says.
*Handmade in limited quantities.* I turn the little box
in my hands. The salt sparkles like an arctic church.
I have to blink against it all.

Tony Hoagland
## THE HEALING PROFESSION


The nurses and orderlies from the hospital
come into the coffee-shop in their blue and green scrubs
with their ID cards on cords around their necks.

They stand in line for their lattes and iced coffee,
checking their phones,
faces bathed in a light cocktail
                    of piano music and air conditioning.

I thought I was destined to spend all my days
trying to get women to take off their clothes
or to win an award for the underachievement
                        of half-formulated goals

but it turns out my vocation was to see
just a few scenes that are presented to me:
the intern whose stethoscope is slung like a necktie

over her left shoulder;
the surgical aide
who hides her bad teeth with a hand.

There is an air that quietly adheres to them
which comes from the ethical work
                    of laying hands on the distressed

so simply to watch them is restful;
simply to observe their flat-soled, practical shoes
                    and casual, resilient mouths

making the shapes of *"Muh"* and *"Oh"*
for *Mocha,*
*"Kuh"* for *Cardiomyopathy.* It is as if,

having squandered one life,
I was swiped clean and given another
                    in which I am allowed to be

the green starched cuff on the orderly's uniform,
tight on his light brown wrist,
                    and how his long, competent fingers

hold the paper cup of Brazilian decaf
into which a lot of milk
and zero-calorie sugar have been stirred.

J. Gerard Chalmers
# I THOUGHT NO ONE WOULD CARE

if I took
nothing more
than warm milk and honey
in the morning and sipped weak
tea in the afternoon.

If I
nibbled
chocolate in the
dark. Kept it wrapped
in wrapping paper stuffed
down into the leather lace-up
boots I never wear, or on the shelf
behind my new Hanukkah doll knowing
the mice might find it if I hid it
under my feather mattress.

I thought no one would care
if I became a girl so thin I
could hide in the silence
of the vestibule
hold my
breath
be invisible, while they
cut tender meat. Buttered fresh bread.

.

Bernadette McBride
# MALLO CUPS

They arrived as a brown-paper cube
tied with string gone greasy with transport
which on removal, showed them glowing
sun-like in red and yellow paper tucked neat

like teeth in the ordered space. I lifted one out
to eat and rushed the rest to the freezer, smacked
with a Scotch-taped sign: *All Mine.* I had, after all,
been the one who'd every day for months bought

with recess money one little square at Silverman's
on the way home from school. The one who'd saved,
according to directions, the collection of cardboard
play money flatted under the brown accordioned cups

in each wrapped package. The one who'd counted
and traded almost daily the 10- and 25-cent coupons
for 5 eventual $1 cards, all that was needed to send
for them. And the one who'd waited for weeks

for the prize to arrive, for the proof all this work
had not been in vain. So, to my 5th-grade way
of thinking they warranted my reasoning,
my hoarding. My first fling at strategized greed.

Ellen Foos
## MADNESS OR CHOCOLATE

Music plays in another room.
It snowed dispiritedly this morning,
the ground outside hard like stale bread.
I'm so sorry for wishing you somewhere else,
the furnace making my head heavy.

Chocolate is the only recourse.
Since the days of feeble Tootsie Rolls,
my enjoyment rides on sweetness.

To dig in a Christmas stocking
is not beyond reason.
I'll spit out a pink taffy center if I must.
It's a biological urge for survival—
one bag of M&Ms at a time.

MaryAnn L. Miller
## PIECES OF DOVE

ride dark in the saddlebag slung
over my shoulder, rest in a laundry
room drawer under the doll clothes,
chill in the freezer's brittle darkness,
slouch behind the pumpernickel,
lurk like a cure in the medicine cabinet
where I used to save cigarettes,

because I know what
it's like to be without at midnight
when the baby is sleeping and
the A&P is closed.

My dry and succulent symbiont
you can't do without me either.

Carl Palmer
## INVITATION FOR COFFEE


*You'll just have to excuse my dirty house*
does not prepare us as she stashes armloads
of clutter behind the food stained couch.

Waiting for us to sit are two large cats
purring intentions of sharing laps and fur
as four or five more meow into the room.

*I hope you both like instant* while wiping
room on her coffee table for three wet cups,
a dusty plastic plate of garlic pretzel mix,

four grey sugar cubes on the Subway napkin
and half empty gallon of fat free milk showing
blue through the month old expiration date.

We rise in unison, brush hair from our slacks,
and reach for our coats almost before we hear
her exclaim, *I can't believe I'm out of coffee.*

Naomi Shihab Nye
# ARABIC COFFEE


It was never too strong for us:
make it blacker, Papa,
thick in the bottom,
tell again how the years will gather
in small white cups,
how luck lives in a spot of grounds.
Leaning over the stove, he let it
boil to the top, and down again.
Two times. No sugar in his pot.
And the place where men and women
break off from one another
was not present in that room.
The hundred disappointments,
fire swallowing olive-wood beads
at the warehouse, and the dreams
tucked like pocket handkerchiefs
into each day, took their places
on the table, near the half-empty
dish of corn. And none was
more important than the others,
and all were guests. When
he carried the tray into the room,
high and balanced in his hands,
it was an offering to all of them,
stay, be seated, follow the talk
wherever it goes. The coffee was
the center of the flower.
Like clothes on a line saying
*you will live long enough to wear me,*
a motion of faith. There is this,
and there is more.

Arlene Weiner
# LETTER FROM HOME

I roasted a chicken Sunday. It was good.
Dad ground Java coffee for breakfast. It was

very good. On Tuesday the first snow
fell, though the leaves are holding on,

and the impatiens was still in bloom.
There had been no frost. A kind October.

Strangers smiled in the street.
For a few moments Tuesday

sun lit the snowflakes and the golden leaves
with the brilliance of three seasons all together.

If you came I would roast a dozen chickens.
Your dad would make a hundred cups of coffee.

I am holding my arms out. If you came
and we were all together

I would not be sad, although the birds
have gone, the impatiens is dead

that pleased strangers all summer. Although dark
comes early now and the seasons can't be stayed.

Sharon Olson
## STILL COOKING AT NINETY-SEVEN


There is life in the batter, the eggs pulling
their weight in a buttery swirl, the spoon
anxious to keep up the circular sweep,
my mother leaning over the pan,
watching the bubbles rising to spout.

She was not an adventurous cook
but no one could match her one discovery,
the gooey factor we might call it.
Simply put in less flour, more sugar,
and the vanilla will speak for itself.

They found her in the kitchen, slumped
on the floor, a procession of attendants
sweet-talking her into the ambulance,
even though *Jeopardy* was about to begin
and her brownies hadn't started to bake.

The doctor explained how the body begins
to break down, the mind disentangling,
whereas chocolate gained sweetness in heat.
We saved the batter and served her brownies
just after we lowered her into the ground.

Virgil Suárez

# TEA LEAVES, *CARACOLES*, COFFEE BEANS

My mother, who in those Havana days believed in divination,
found her tea leaves at *El Volcán*, the Chinese market/apothecary,

brought the leaves in a precious silk paper bundle, unwrapped
them as if unwrapping her own skin, and then boiled water

to make my dying grandmother's tea; while my mother read
its leaves, I simply saw *leaves floating* in steaming water,

vapor kissed my skin, my nose became moist as a puppy's.
My mother did this because my grandmother, her mother-in-law,

believed in all things. Her appetite for knowledge was vast,
the one thing we all agreed she passed down to me, the skinny

kid sent to search for *caracoles*, these snail shells
that littered the underbrush of the empty lot next door.

My mother threw them on top of the table, cleaned them of dirt,
kept them in a mason jar and every morning before breakfast,

read them on top of the table, their way of falling, some up,
some down, their ridges, swirls of creamy lines, their broken

edges…. Everything she read looked bad, for my grandmother,
for us, for staying in our country, this island of suspended

disbelief. My mother read coffee beans too, with their wrinkled,
fleshy green and red skin. Orange-skinned beans she kept aside.

Orange meant death, and my mother didn't want to accept it.
I learned mostly of death from the way a sparrow fell

when I hit it in the chest with my slingshot and a lead pellet
I made by melting toy soldiers. The sparrow's eyes

always hid behind droopy eyelids, which is how my grandmother
died, by closing her eyes to the world; truth became this fading

light, a tunnel, as everybody says, but instead of heaven
she went into the ground, to that one place that still nourishes

the tea leaves, *caracoles*, and the coffee beans, which, if I didn't
know better, I'd claim shone; those red-glowing beans

in starlight were the eyes of the dead looking out through
the darkness as those of us who believed in such things walked

through life with a lightness of feet, spirit, a vapor-aura
that could be read or sung.

Carolina Morales
# COFFEE POT


Handed down from the far corner
of a kitchen cabinet in the terminal
month after his death, I receive
its muted cast, rub its reflective side,
conjure a mirror of the past, shards
of my face refracted
in the lid's glass knob, steam circling
from the lip, beams leavened through
windows that once defined
a kitchen wall, settled across linoleum floor,
spread to the leafless Formica table where
we sat, my mother's hands, her gold
banded finger cupped around
the tempered pot now placed
beside a set of aluminum trays,
wedding gifts I am told, presented
at their start, before the boil
and quick dissolve of their marriage,
bitter aftertaste, grind of their daily lives
into each watery death.
When he moved out, I suppose
he took the things he wanted:
the pot; the trays; a brown cache
of photographs; a hand mixer,
Hamilton Beach, ironclad; left
behind a woman stumbling
with three children,

an apartment due a full month's rent,
a daughter who equates a coffee pot
resistant to corrosion with found treasure,
holds the seeped aroma drifting
from its metal well against
the sharp bite of sediments,
strains of its dark brew.

Amy Lemmon
## ENJOY HOT OR ICED


You've brewed this stuff, now drink it—
these dreggy-dregs, this filter-silt,
the tiny bits that cling to tongue.
You always liked it strong and now
you've got it at its darkest, split
us at the core to brew a full bold flavor,
so each must shoulder/bear the double-weight
of everything except the other's body.
I hope you have your fun and drink it, too,
iced now as much as it was hot. I don't. I didn't
order it this way. I wanted café au lait,
and when the waiter brought it and I asked for water,
he said flat "No" and mugged—a joke, I thought,
but sure enough, he never brought a glass, left me
to fend with froth and squeeze a dollar tip. He thought
he was funny. You think you're kind, you think
you're sensible, you think you're something
I can't quite imagine. What of the Monet's
lily-pads of mold on Earl Grey cooling in the jar?
The brown scrub-nulling scum that clings
to the worn Picasso mug? The ghosts of shattered crockery,
the cartoon souls of slain French press carafes?
Yours, yours, mine, ours. It's a toss-up,
so you clay-pigeon it again and pull! Shoot! A hit!
My heart, I mean, that flat and battered thing
you had and lately thought so little of.

# AFTERLIFE

Believe me, there's no metaphysics on earth like chocolates.

—Fernando Pessoa, "The Tobacco Shop"

Carol V. Davis
## CHOCOLATE AND THE AFTERLIFE

She wrote of it as no one had: of the men who picked the pods,
dried the beans, ground the nibs, walked home trailing a scent
from the walls of Hansel and Gretel, all the way to the Aztecs and
Mayans. She hovered in kitchens, dipped her fingers in blackened
pots, stacked the recipes, shuffled them skillfully as a poker player.
Her cookbook was proclaimed the bible of all bibles. It bought
her the land, built the house, paid for a redwood deck, polished
to the color of cinnamon. But restlessness nipped at her. Travel
caught her in its hot-air balloon. Chocolate soufflés deflated as she
moved on. Next a stampede of wolfhounds with eyes one step
from the tundra. She trusted them. Whippets sleek as shadows
moved in; she rescued borzois, found homes for the neglected.
Any four-legged creature, even as she abandoned friends. I hadn't
seen her for years when I got the call, standing at the counter
chopping dill. I'll rifle my cupboard for bitter chocolate, melt it
down, pour it from on high, a dark river to the afterlife.

Lynn Shapiro
## TWO OR THREE THINGS I KNOW ABOUT COFFEE*

> *The swirling surface of a cup of coffee is transformed into the*
> *primordial ooze and also the infinite universe.*
>
> —Amy Taubin

Stir, silver conducts best
*maybe an object is what serves as a link between subjects*
you are the filmmaker now and metaphor is at your table
*allowing us to live in society, to be together*
try a loud whisper for intimacy, stress "s" sounds
*but since social relations are always ambiguous,*
like the hiss of foaming milk
*since my thoughts divide as much as unite*
be distracted
*and my words unite by what they express and isolate*
what just flew by?
*by what they omit since a wide gulf separates my subjective certainty*
sip, stop, read
*of myself from the objective truth others have of me*
look into your cup, wander
*since I constantly end up guilty even though I feel innocent,*
    *since every event changes my daily life,*
the coffee is too bitter
*since I always fail to communicate, to understand, to love and be loved,*
but I appreciate you preparing it for me
*and every failure deepens my solitude, since ....*
I sit and ponder over the morning news
*since...I cannot escape the objectivity crushing me nor the subjectivity*
    *expelling me,*
trapped in my own cup
*since I cannot rise to a state of being nor collapse into nothingness...*

I can find everything at my fingertips
*I have to listen, more than ever, I have to look around me,*
    *at my world, my fellow creature, my brother*
Drink in


*Italics indicate voiceover from Jean-Luc Godard's film *Two or Three Things
I Know About Her*

Michael Fitzgerald-Clarke
## 3047


In 3047, what of soul? I have
a chocolate heart and coffee through my
veins, and I am a philosopher and I
ask—is this pure?

Soft tech is passé;—we experience being
eaten by ants & birds, & our bodies
always are slightly broken.

Take a handful of your heart,
make a cake with it, and offer
it to sacred being. Nothing else
can distil faux tragedy or

stop us, yet again, from something
metaphorical, like continued life. My
heart is soothed ahead of time

and my mood has changed. I cherish
connectedness; to fire and its ash;
to separateness full flavoured two
hours after midnight;

I skirt, and gamble chocolate squares
and milk espressos until I'm ringed by
daze, days.

Let what you believe be soft in your
hands. I am here, concocted, and named
meltingly for heaven.

Suzanne Lummis
## TWO CUPS

*I don't like coffee—it makes me think of death.*
— Gabriel García Márquez

i.
Yes
but only if you gaze down
as into the round black
mouth of a
well where a tossed
coin
never stops
turning
heads
tails
heads and the clasped
dark leans
against the gypsy
lines of your palms
and the result of
the toss your fortune your
life that Wish-in-
Nose-Dive is far
gone still
falling

ii.
Yes but only if you gaze
down through your own

hands cupped like a
beggar's with a circle
of dark at the center like
the pipeline or porthole
keyhole
to a shadow world
because you've stayed up
all night on nothing
but blues and black
coffee and the sound
of windy traffic
outside your door
which reminds you
of death or is that
the coffee?

To be safe pour your
self another bottomless cup
as they used to say in
the diners and don't
sleep.

Charles Simic
# WATCH REPAIR

A small wheel
Incandescent,
Shivering like
A pinned butterfly.

Hands thrown up
In all directions:
The crossroads
One arrives at
In a nightmare.

Higher than that
Number 12 presides
Like a beekeeper
Over the swarming honeycomb
Of the open watch.

Other wheels
That could fit
Inside a raindrop.

Tools
That must be splinters
Of arctic starlight.

Tiny golden mills
Grinding invisible
Coffee beans.

When the coffee's boiling
Cautiously,
So it doesn't burn us,
We raise it
To the lips
Of the nearest
Ear.

Michael Palmer
## THE COUNTER-SKY

A young woman of the book
directed my gaze toward the counter-sky

Behind her there were books piled up
miles and miles of books piled high

and below the scholars bent to their tasks
reading by the light of green-tinted lamps

I stared at the coffee in my cup
the coffee in my empty cup

and asked, "Would you like
a sip of coffee from this cup?"

And she said yes, and drink she did
from my cup's perfect emptiness.

Tomas Tranströmer
## ESPRESSO

Black coffee at sidewalk cafes
With chairs and tables like gaudy insects.

It is a precious sip we intercept
Filled with the same strength as Yes and No.

It is fetched out of gloomy kitchens
And looks into the sun without blinking.

In daylight a dot of wholesome black
Quickly drained by the wan patron...

Like those black drops of profundity
Sometimes absorbed by the soul

That give us a healthy push: Go!
The courage to open our eyes.

*Translated from the Swedish by May Swenson and Leif Sjöberg*

## ACKNOWLEDGMENTS

Grateful acknowledgment is made to the publications where some of the poems were first printed. Unless specifically noted otherwise, copyright of the poems is held by the individual poets.

Dannie Abse: "Chocolate Box" from *Be Seated, Thou: Poems 1989–1998*, © 2000 by Dannie Abse, used by permission of The Sheep Meadow Press, www. sheepmeadowpress.org.

Jennifer Arin: "Xocolatl" from *Ways We Hold* by Jennifer Arin (Dos Madres, 2012). Reprinted by permission of the author.

Catherine Barnett: "Acts of Mind" is from a forthcoming collection (Graywolf Press, 2016). Reprinted by permission of the author.

Richard Brautigan: "Xerox Candy Bar" from *The Pill Versus the Springhill Mine Disaster* by Richard Brautigan. Copyright © 1968 by Richard Brautigan. Reproduced by permission of Houghton Mifflin Harcourt Publishing Company. All rights reserved.

Mary Cheever: from *The Need for Chocolate & Other Poems* (Stein & Day, 1980), by permission of the estate of Mary W. Cheever.

Susan Cohen: "Reportorial" first appeared in *Harpur Palate* (Jan. 29, 2014).

Carol V. Davis: "Chocolate and the Afterlife" was first published in *The Prose-Poem Project*, Fall 2010, and then in *Between Storms* by Carol V. Davis (Truman State University Press, 2012).

Elaine Equi: "Ciao Bella Chocolate Sorbet" from *Ripple Effect: New and Selected Poems* © 2007 by Elaine Equi, used by permission of Coffee House Press, www.coffeehousepress.org.

R.G. Evans: "In the Café at the End of the World" from *Overtipping the Ferryman* by R.G. Evans (Aldrich Press, 2014). Reprinted by permission of the author.

Ellen Foos: "Madness or Chocolate" from *Little Knitted Sister* by Ellen Foos (Ragged Sky Press, 2006).

Dorothea Grossman: "I allow myself" reprinted by permission from *The Fun of Speaking English*, by Dorothea Grossman (Coffeetown Press, 2012).

# ABOUT THE POETS

**Dannie Abse** was a poet, author, doctor and playwright. He wrote and edited more than sixteen books of poetry, as well as fiction and a range of other publications. He is the author of *Ash on a Young Man's Sleeve* and several autobiographical volumes, the most recent of which, *Goodbye, Twentieth Century*, was published by Pimlico in 2001 to critical acclaim. His most recent novel, *The Strange Case of Dr Simmonds & Dr Glas*, was published in 2002 and long-listed for the Booker Prize. In 2003 his *New and Collected Poems* received the Special Commendation of the Poetry Book Society, and his book of poetry, *Running Late* received the Roland Mathais Prize in 2007. His most recent book of poetry, *Ask the Moon* was published November 2014.

**Jennifer Arin** is the author of the poetry collection *Ways We Hold* (2012), and her writings have been published in both the United States and Europe, including in *The AWP Writer's Chronicle, The San Francisco Chronicle Sunday Book Review, Gastronomica, Puerto del Sol, Poet Lore, ZYZZYVA, Chain, Paris/Atlantic Review,* and *The Chronicle of Higher Education*, among others. Recent awards include a grant from the National Endowment for the Humanities, a PEN Writer's Fund grant, a Poets & Writers Writers-On-Site Residency, and funding from the Spanish Ministry of Culture. She teaches in the English Department at San Francisco State University.

**Catherine Barnett** is the author of *The Game of Boxes* (Graywolf Press), which won the 2012 James Laughlin Award, and *Into Perfect Spheres Such Holes Are Pierced* (Alice James Books, 2004). Her honors include a Whiting Writer's Award and a Guggenheim Fellowship. She teaches in graduate programs at NYU, Hunter College, and the New School. She also works as an independent editor and has degrees from Princeton University, where she will be teaching this year, and from the MFA Program for Writers at Warren Wilson College.

**Richard Gary Brautigan** was an American novelist, poet, and short story writer. His work often employs black comedy, parody, and satire. He is best known for his 1967 novel *Trout Fishing in America*.

**Carol Buckley** lives in San Diego, California, and works at the Athenaeum Music & Arts Library in nearby La Jolla and has a freelance editing business. She also writes periodically for newsletters. Other poems of hers have been published in the *Magee Park Poets Anthology*. She is a member of the Gypsy Poets, and their chapbook was recently on view at the San Diego Central Public Library.

**Chris Bullard** is a native of Jacksonville, Florida. He lives in Collingswood, New Jersey and works for the federal goverment as an Administrative Law Judge. He received a BA in English from the University of Pennsylvania and a MFA in Creative Writing from Wilkes University. Plan B Press published his first chapbook, *You Must Not Know Too Much*, in 2009. Big Table Publishing published his second chapbook, *O Brilliant Kids,* in 2011. WordTech Published *Back*, his first full-length book, in November 2013.

**J. Gerard Chalmers** is a New York writer and photographer with an MFA from Columbia University. She has published poems, reviews and social *commentary* in many literary publications such as *Bellevue Literary Review, Barrow Street, New Millennium Writing, Fogged Clarity, Chelsea, Inkwell,* and the *Kenyon Review* (online). She was nominated for the 2014 anthology, *Best New Poets*. Chalmers attended the Colrain Poetry Manuscript Conference in 2013 and 2014. She is currently working on a series of poems about Picasso's mistress, the artist Dora Maar.

**Mary Cheever, a** poet, artist and teacher, taught writing for a time; wrote a history of Briarcliff Manor, New York; and in 1980 published a book, *The Need for Chocolate & Other Poems*. She was the widow of the writer John Cheever and they had three children. She lived in Ossining, New York, and died there in 2014 at the age of 95.

**Susan Cohen** is a journalist who has won numerous honors. She was at one time on the faculty of the Graduate School of Journalism at the University of California, Berkeley, and has since become a contributing writer to the *Washington Post Magazine* and a book reviewer and columnist. Her poems have appeared in many literary journals, including: *Atlanta Review, Connecticut Review, Harpur Palate, Hunger Mountain, Poetry East, Poetry International, Poet Lore,* and *Valparaiso Poetry Review*. In 2012, Cherry Grove Collections (WordTech) published her first full-length book of poems, *Throat Singing*.

**Elizabeth Danson** was born in India, spent her early childhood in China, and was educated in England. She has lived in the United States for most of her adult life. She has taught, worked in publishing, and administered an arts center. Her writing has appeared in the *New Yorker, U.S.1 Worksheets, The New Review, Fourth Genre, Anon One,* and her first collection, *The Luxury of Obstacles*, was published in 2006 (Ragged Sky Press).

**Carol Davis** is the author of the full-length poetry collections *It's Time to Talk About… / Pora Govorit'o*—(1997), a bilingual collection published in Russia; *Into the Arms of Pushkin: Poems of St. Petersburg* (2007), winner of the T.S. Eliot Prize; and *Between Storm* (2012). Her chapbooks include *Letters from Prague* (1991) *and The Violin Teacher* (2005). As a senior Fulbright scholar from 1996 to 1997, Davis taught at Petersburg Jewish University in St. Petersburg. In 2008, she was poet-in-residence at Olivet College in Michigan. She teaches at Santa Monica College in California.

**Theodore Eisenberg** recently retired from the practice of labor law after 38 years. He is writing poetry full-time.

**Elaine Equi** received a BA and an MA in English from Columbia College, where she taught a poetry workshop for several years after graduating. Along with her husband, Jerome Sala, she was active in Chicago's performance poetry scene. Equi's first book, *Federal Woman*, was published in 1978 by Danaides Press. She has written over ten books of poetry including, *Voice-Over* (1999), chosen by Thom Gunn for the San Francisco State Poetry Award, *The Cloud of Knowable Things* (2003), *Ripple Effect: New and Selected Poems* (2007), which was shortlisted for the 2008 International Griffin Poetry Prize, and *Click and Clone* (2011), and *Sentences and Rain* (forthcoming) all from Coffee House Press.

**R.G. Evans** is the author of *Overtipping the Ferryman* (Aldrich Press Award 2013). His poems, reviews, and fiction have appeared in *Rattle*, *Pif Magazine*, *Tiferet*, *The Literary Review*, and *Weird Tales*, as well as other journals. His original music, including the song "The Crows of Paterson," was featured in the 2012 documentary *All That Lies Between Us*. Evans has read his poems at the 2014 Geraldine R. Dodge Festival and the 2015 Bridgewater International Poetry Festival. He teaches high school and college English and Creative Writing in southern New Jersey.

**Joan Fishbein's** work has appeared in the *Origami Poems Project of Rhode Island*, *The Southern Poetry Anthology: Volume One*, *The Kennesaw Review*, *The Devil's Millhopper*, *Helicon Nine*, *Poetica*, *The Reach of Song*, *New Verse News*, *Of Sun and Sand Anthology*, and other small literary magazines. She won first prize for poetry at the 2008 Chattahoochee Valley Writers' Conference and has writing forthcoming in a nine-person chapbook published by Main Street Rag.

**Michael Fitzgerald-Clarke** is an Australian poet writing from Townsville in tropical North Queensland. If he could have one wish, he would give that wish away.

**Ellen Foos** is a senior production editor for Princeton University Press. She is the founder and publisher of Ragged Sky Press and was the recipient of fellowships to the MacDowell Colony and the Vermont Studio Center. She coedited *Eating Her Wedding Dress: A Collection of Clothing Poems*, and her first collection of poems, *Little Knitted Sister*, was published in 2006. Her poetry has appeared in *U.S. 1 Worksheets*, *The Kelsey Review*, *Edison Literary Review*, and *Contemporary American Voices*.

A native of Philadelphia, **Dorothea "Dottie" Grossman** lived in Los Angeles for thirty-plus years. Her work was featured in the March, 2010 edition of *Poetry* magazine and was awarded that magazine's J. Howard and Barbara M. J. Wood Prize. The 2007 opera, *Five*, by flutist/producer Ellen Burr, is based on a selection of her poems. Her work has appeared in numerous poetry journals and magazines. Grossman published four poetry collections: *The Fun of Speaking English: Selected Poems* (Coffeetown Press), *Cuttings* and *Poems From Cave 17* (self-published), and *Museum of Rain* (Take Out Press). Her two CDs, *Call & Response* and *Call & Response & Friends*, represent the poet in live performance mode with improvising musicians. Dorothea Grossman died on May 6, 2012 at the age of 75.

**Lois Marie Harrod's** 13th and 14th poetry collections, *Fragments from the Biography of Nemesis* (Cherry Grove Press) and the chapbook *How Marlene Mae Longs for Truth* (Dancing Girl Press) appeared in 2013. *The Only Is* won the 2012 Tennessee Chapbook Contest (Poems & Plays), and *Brief Term*, a collection of poems about teachers and teaching, was published by Black Buzzard Press, 2011. *Cosmogony* won the 2010 Hazel Lipa Chapbook (Iowa State). She is widely published in literary journals and online ezines from *American Poetry Review* to *Zone 3*. She teaches Creative Writing at The College of New Jersey.

**Ishmael von Heidrick-Barnes** is author of *Intimate Geography: Poems* (Ragged Sky Press, 2012), winner of the San Diego Book Award for poetry. He is editor of the *Magee Park Poets Anthology*. Ishmael studied Religion and Theology at the University of San Diego, and holds a degree in Surgical Technology. He collaborates with German sculptor Roger Rigorth and writes lyrics for opera singer Andrea Hoerkens. Ishmael's visual art has been published in journals and is incorporated into his readings.

**Carlos Hernández Peña** is the author of *Moonmilk and Other Poems* (Ragged Sky Press, 2006). He has also served as a coeditor of the *U.S.1 Worksheets* magazine, and organized *Voices* at the Princeton Public Library, a biannual program of poetry from around the world presented in a bilingual format. His work has appeared in *Drunken Boat*, *The Fox Chase Review*, and *Princeton Magazine*, as well as *US1 Worksheets*. His translations into Spanish include: *Under the Southern Cross* (from the English translation of the Hungarian, in an illustrated limited edition, 2012) and *Fortino Sámano* (from the French, forthcoming). Carlos works for The Segal Company, employee benefit consultants and actuaries in Princeton, New Jersey.

**Tony Hoagland's** books of poetry include *Sweet Ruin* (1992); *Donkey Gospel* (1998), winner of the James Laughlin Award; *What Narcissism Means to Me* (2003), a finalist for the National Book Critics Circle Award; *Rain* (2005); and *Unincorporated Persons in the Late Honda Dynasty* (2010). He has also published a collection of essays about poetry, *Real Sofistakashun* (2006). Hoagland's many honors and awards include fellowships from the National Endowment for the Arts and the Provincetown Fine Arts Work Center. He has received the O.B. Hardison Prize for Poetry and Teaching from the Folger Shakespeare Library, the Poetry Foundation's Mark Twain Award and the Jackson Poetry Prize from *Poets & Writers*. Hoagland teaches at the University of Houston and in the Warren Wilson MFA program.

drianne **Kalfopoulou** lives and teaches in Athens, Greece, where she is currently on
e faculty of Hellenic American University. She has taught in the Scottish Universities'
ternational Summer Schools Program at the University of Edinburgh, and is part of the
junct faculty in the Creative Writing Program at New York University, and various
eative writing workshops in Greece. Her scholarly work has focused on nineteenth-
d twentieth-century American literature, particularly the contributions of Nathaniel
awthorne, Margaret Fuller, Toni Morrison and Marilynne Robinson. She is currently
mpleting a collection of essays, and is at work on a monograph that explores Ralph
aldo Emerson's influence on Sylvia Plath's poems.

siliki **Katsarou's** poems have appeared in *Agave Magazine, Poetry Daily, Regime*
trnal (Australia), *wicked alice, Wild River Review*, as well as in the anthologies *Rabbit
rs: TV Poems* (NYQ Books), and *Not Somewhere Else But Here: A Contemporary
ithology of Women and Place.* Her first collection, *Memento Tsunami*, was published in 2011
d one of its poems was nominated for a Pushcart Prize. Vasiliki was one of
venty national and international poets to read work at the 2014 Dodge Poetry Festival,
e largest poetry festival in the United States. She founded and directs the Panoply Books
eading Series in Lambertville, New Jersey. More about her poetry can be found at
tp://www.onegoldbead.com/.

2014 Dean **Kostos's** book, *This Is Not a Skyscraper*, won the Benjamin Saltman Poetry
ward, selected by Mark Doty and was published by Red Hen Press in March of 2015.
ostos is the author of the following collections: *Rivering, Last Supper of the Senses, The
ntence That Ends with a Comma*, and *Celestial Rust*. He was also the coeditor of *Mama's
y: Gay Men Write about Their Mothers* (a Lambda Book Award finalist) and the editor
*Pomegranate Seeds: An Anthology of Greek-American Poetry.* His poems, personal essays,
d reviews have appeared in *Barrow Street, Boulevard, Chelsea, Cimarron Review, New
adrid, Southwest Review, Stand Magazine, Talisman, Western Humanities Review*, on Oprah
infrey's Web site oxygen.com, the Harvard University Press website, and in many
er leading journals. His poem "Subway Silk" was translated into a film by Canadian
nmaker Jill Clark.

ny **Lemmon** is the author of the poetry collections *Fine Motor* (Sow's Ear Poetry Press
08) and *Saint Nobody* (Red Hen 2009). Her poems and essays have appeared in
lling Stone, New Letters, Prairie Schooner, Verse, Barrow Street, Court Green*, the *Journal,
rginalia*, and many other magazines and anthologies. A Pushcart Prize nominee, she has
ntributed articles to the *Greenwood Encyclopedia of American Poets and Poetry* and the *Facts
File Companion to Twentieth-Century British Poetry. ABBA: The Poems*, a chapbook Amy
ote collaboratively with Denise Duhamel, is forthcoming from Coconut Books. Amy
lds a PhD in English and creative writing from the University of Cincinnati and is the
ipient of scholarships from the Vermont Studio Center, Sewanee Writers' Conference,

West Chester Poetry Conference, and Antioch Writers' Workshop. An associate professor and assistant chair of the English and Speech Department at New York's Fashion Institute of Technology, she lives in Astoria, Queens, with her two children.

**Suzanne Lummis'** book, *Open 24 Hours*, received the Blue Lynx Poetry Prize. Her poems have appeared in *The New Yorker, Ploughshares, The Antioch Review* and other notable journals. She is an influential teacher, writer and performer in the Los Angeles region and a principal exponent of the "poem noir."

**Bernadette McBride** is the author of *Waiting for the Light to Change* published by WordTech Press (2013) and *Food, Wine, and Other Essential Considerations–an Alphabet*, published by Aldrich Press (2014). She is on the English faculty of Temple University where she teaches American and Women's Literature, poetry and fiction writing, and she teaches college writing and literature at Bucks County Community College. She also writes essays and short stories, and includes journalism in her background.

**Amy Miller's** poetry has appeared in *Nimrod, Northwest Review, Rattle, Willow Springs,* and *ZYZZYVA*, and is upcoming in the anthologies *The Knotted Bond: Oregon Poets Speak of Their Sisters* and *London Calling: A Clash Anthology*. She was a finalist for the Pablo Neruda Prize and 49th Parallel Award, and won the Cultural Center of Cape Cod National Poetry Competition, judged by Tony Hoagland. She lives in Ashland, Oregon, where she works as the publications manager for the Oregon Shakespeare Festival and blogs at writers–island.blogspot.com.

**MaryAnn L. Miller** holds an M.Ed, an MFA from Rosemont College, and completed a Postgraduate semester with the poet David Wojahn at Vermont College of Fine Arts. Miller's book of poems, *Locus Mentis*, has been published by PS Books. She has been published in *Philadelphia Poets Anthology, Certain Circuits, The International Review of African American Art, The Fox Chase Review, Rathalla Review, Musehouse Journal*, and *Kaleidoscope*. Her poems and serigraphs were published in the September 2013 issue of *Wordgathering*. She was the Resident Book Artist at the Experimental Printmaking Institute, Lafayette College for twelve years, where she taught workshops in book arts and letterpress. Her work is in the National Museum of Women in the Arts and in many corporate and private collections. She publishes hand-bound artist books pairing artists and poets through her press: www.luciapress.com. Miller hosts a Poetry Series at the Hunterdon Art Museum in Clinton, New Jersey, and teaches a workshop in the Poetry of Visual Art.

**Carolina Morales** is the author of three collections of poetry, *Bride of Frankenstein and Other Poems* (2008), *In Nancy Drew's Shadow* (2010) and *Dear Monster* (2012), each published by Finishing Line Press. Her poems have appeared in *Coal City Review, Kelsey*

*Review, Journal of New Jersey Poets, Nimrod, Paterson Literary Review, Poet Lore, Schuylkill Valley Journal, Spoon River Poetry Review, U.S. 1 Worksheets* and other journals and anthologies. Three of Carolina's poems have been nominated for Pushcart prizes. She is a past recipient of a scholarship from the summer program at the Fine Arts Work Center in Provincetown, Massachusetts, and in 2011, Carolina's short play, *The Last December*, was produced by Fire Rose Productions in North Hollywood, California. In 2014, an excerpt of her full-length play, *Ladies Man*, was given a staged reading as part of the New Voices program at the Bucks County Playhouse in New Hope, Pennsylvania.

**Sharon Olson** is a retired librarian, a graduate of Stanford, with an MLS from U.C. Berkeley and an MA in Comparative Literature from the University of Oregon. Her book *The Long Night of Flying* was published by Sixteen Rivers Press in 2006. Her poems have appeared in such journals as *Crab Orchard Review, Arroyo Literary Review, U.S. 1 Worksheets, Off the Coast,* and *Cider Press Review,* which nominated one of her poems for a Pushcart Prize. She currently lives in Lawrenceville, New Jersey.

**Coco Owen** is a stay-at-home poet in Los Angeles. She has published in the *Antioch Review, The Journal, 1913, Cirque, Tidal Basin Review* and Rio Grande Review, among others, and has a mini-chapbook with Binge Press. Owen is on Les Figues Press's board of directors, curates their literary salon, Mrs. Porter's, and last worked at Reed College. More of her work can be found at: www.cocoowenphd.com.

**Carl "Papa" Palmer**, retired Army, retired FAA, now just plain retired, lives in University Place, Washington. He has seven chapbooks and a contest-winning poem riding a bus somewhere in Seattle. Motto: Long Weekends Forever.

**Michael Palmer** was born in New York City in 1943. He is the recipient of two grants from the Literature Program of the National Endowment for the Arts, and was a Guggenheim Fellow in 1989–90. He has written eight books of poetry and is often published in such literary magazines as *Boundary 2, Berkeley Poetry Review, Sulfur, Conjunctions,* and *O-blek.* His most recent books of poetry are *At Passages* (1996) and *The Lion Bridge: Selected Poems 1972–1995* (1998), both published by New Directions. He presently lives in San Francisco, California

**Niki Petrosino** is the author of two books of poetry: *Hymn for the Black Terrific* (2013) and *Fort Red Border* (2009), both from Sarabande Books. She holds graduate degrees from the University of Chicago and the University of Iowa Writer's Workshop. Her poems have appeared in *Best American Poetry,* the *New York Times, FENCE, Gulf Coast, Jubilat, Tin House* and elsewhere. She is founder and coeditor of Transom, an independent on-line poetry journal. She is an Associate Professor of English at the University of Louisville, where she directs the Creative Writing Program.

**James Richardson** is a professor of English and Creative Writing at Princeton University. His books include *Thomas Hardy: The Poetry of Necessity, Vanishing Lives: Style and Self in Tennyson, Rossetti, Swinburne and Yeats* and several volumes of poetry and aphorisms, including *Interglacial: New and Selected Poems and Aphorisms,* which was a finalist for the 2004 National Book Critics Circle Award, and *Vectors: Aphorisms and Ten-Second Essays.* He has recent poems and aphorisms in *Best American Poetry, New Yorker, Slate, Yale Review, Paris Review, Science News,* and *Poetry Daily.*

**Hayden Saunier** is the author of two poetry collections, *Tips for Domestic Travel* (Black Lawrence Press) and *Say Luck* (Big Pencil Press) which won the 2013 Gell Poetry Prize. Her work has been widely published and awarded the 2011 Pablo Neruda Prize, the 2011 Rattle Poetry Prize and the 2005 Robert Fraser Award for Poetry.

**Therese Sellers** is a Hellenist who specializes in teaching Ancient Greek to young children. Her first book, *Alpha is for Anthropos,* is a collection of nursery rhymes she composed in Greek to be sung to the tune of familiar children's songs. Therese is a prolific haiku poet and has published over six hundred haiku on Twitter. She is bringing these poems out in print as a series of chapbooks, organized by theme. The first in the series, *Advent Calendar Haiku,* came out in 2014. Therese is currently working on an English translation of *Aioliki Yi* by Ilias Venezis, a lyrical account of the author's childhood in Asia Minor before World War I. Therese lives in New England and dreams of Greece.

**Lynne Shapiro** is a writer and teacher who lives with her husband and son in Hoboken, New Jersey. She loves birds and ferns, hats and earrings, surrealists and minimalists. She's had poems and essays published recently in *Myslexia, Trespass, Terrain. org,* and *Umbrella.*

**Naomi Shihab** Nye was born to an American mother and a Palestinian father. At the age of 14, her family moved to Jerusalem. Upon returning to the United States, she earned a BA from Trinity University in 1974. She is the author of several books of poems, including *19 Varieties of Gazelle: Poems of the Middle East* (2002), *Fuel* (1998), and *Red Suitcase* (1994). Nye has received the Texas Institute of Letters award, the Charity Randall prize, the Paterson Poetry Prize, and four Pushcart Prizes. She also writes book for children. She lives today in San Antonio, Texas, with her husband and son.

**Charles Simic** is a poet, essayist, and translator. He is the recipient of many awards, including the Pulitzer Prize, the Griffin Prize, and a MacArthur Fellowship. In 2007 Simic was appointed the fifteenth Poet Laureate Consultant in Poetry to the Library of Congress. *The Lunatic,* his new volume of poetry, and *The Life of Images,* a book of his selected prose, were published in April 2015.

**Jody Struve** works for the Robert Wood Johnson Foundation. She received her BA, summa cum laude, from Rider College. Born in Chicago, she and her wife, Erinn Auletta, a middle school teacher, live in Lambertville, New Jersey, with their two young children.

**Virgil Suárez** left Cuba with his family when he was just 12. Eventually settling in the United States, he earned a BA from California State University, Long Beach, and an MFA from Louisiana State University and is currently an associate professor of creative writing at Florida State University in Tallahassee. In both his poetry and his prose, Suárez seeks to capture the experience of migration. Suárez connects his personal experience as an immigrant with larger themes of identity, history, and language.

**Maxine Susman's** work appears in dozens of journals and anthologies *(Paterson Literary Review, U.S. 1 Worksheets, Ekphrasis, Earth's Daughters, Comstock Review, Poet Lore)*. She has won awards from the Allen Ginsberg Poetry Contest and many other contests. Maxine has published four poetry collections: *Gogama* (2006), *Wartime Address* (2009), *Familiar* 2009) and *Creamery Road* (2011). She taught literature and writing for many years at Rutgers, Seton Hall, Caldwell College, and Duksung Women's University in Seoul, Korea. Newly retired from her job as Professor of English at Caldwell, she continues there as Poet in Residence. A member of the poetry performance group Cool Women, she recently moved from Highland Park to the Princeton area.

Australian-born **Katrin Talbot** has a forthcoming volume, *noun'd, verb* (dancing girl press) and two collections: *Freeze-Dried Love* (Finishing Line Press) and *St. Cecilia's Daze* (Parallel Press). She has recently been nominated for two chocolate- and coffee-fueled Pushcart Prizes and once received enough prize money from a national poetry contest to fund a Dairy Queen run.

**Tomas Tranströmer**, one of Sweden's leading poets, studied poetry and psychology at the University of Stockholm. His numerous collections of poetry include *Windows and Stones* (1972), an International Poetry Forum Selection and runner-up for the National Book Award for translation, and *The Great Enigma: New Collected Poems* (2006, 2011), translated by Robin Fulton. His longstanding friendship with poet Robert Bly, who has also translated and edited some of his work, is documented in *Air Mail* (2001), a collection of more than 25 years of their correspondence. Tranströmer, who died in 2015, has also published a memoir, *Minnena Ser Mig (Memories Look At Me*, 1993). He won the Nobel Prize in Literature in 2011.

**BJ Ward** grew up in New Jersey. He earned a BA at Richard Stockton College of New Jersey and an MA at Syracuse University. He is the author of several collections of poetry, including *Jackleg Opera: Collected Poems 1990 to 2013; Gravedigger's Birthday* (2002), a Paterson Poetry Prize finalist; *17 Love Poems With No Despair* (1997); and

*Landing in New Jersey with Soft Hands* (1994). His poems have been featured on Garrison Keillor's National Public Radio program *The Writer's Almanac*, and he has received fellowships from the Geraldine R. Dodge Foundation, the New Jersey State Council on the Arts, and the Artist/Teacher Institute, as well as a Pushcart Prize. He has taught at the Frost Place Seminar for Young Poets, the New Jersey Governor's School for the Arts, and Warren County Community College.

**Arlene Weiner** has worked as college instructor, cardiology technician, research associate in educational software, and editor. She grew up in Inwood, near Manhattan's northern tip, and has lived in Massachusetts, California, Princeton, and Pittsburgh. Her first collection of poetry, *Escape Velocity*, came out in 2006. A MacDowell fellow, her poems have appeared in *The Louisville Review; Pleiades, a Journal of New Writing; Poet Lore; U.S. 1 newspaper;* and *U.S. 1 Worksheets.*

While in high school **Rosemary O'Neil Wright** read a quote from Dylan Thomas, "Poetry is not the same as prayer, but it arises from the same need." The words resonated with her and she has been reading poetry ever since. Rosemary earned an MA in Education from Stanford University and taught high school mathematics for twenty years. After her retirement she began taking writing classes at Brookdale Community College where she had several poems published in the literary magazine. Rosemary is now enrolled in the Monmouth University MA Program in Creative Writing. Rosemary has also been a professional storyteller for over twenty-five years. She performs at festivals, banquets, and libraries. She is a member of the Garden State Storytellers League and the New Jersey Storytelling Network, and has organized a new group of storytellers at the Jersey Shore called Storytellers Mosaic.

**Ruth Zamoyta** coeditor of *Blanket Stories*, is also is the author of *'Otsu' and Other Poems* (2007, Bronze by Gold) and *clarissa@loveless.com* (2002, classicnovels.com), and the coeditor, with Ellen Foos and Vasiliki Katsarou, of *Eating Her Wedding Dress: A Collection of Clothing Poems* (2009, Ragged Sky Press), which features her poem, "My Bra." She lives in the New York City area where she develops strategies and runs projects for art and education non-profits by day, and fences épée by night.

## NOTE

The anthology's title comes from *Eyes and Ears*, a collection of letters by Henry Ward Beecher published in1862. Henry Ward Beecher was a social reformer and the brother of Harriet Beecher Stowe.

*"A cup of coffee—real coffee—home-browned, home ground, home made, that comes to you dark as a hazel-eye, but changes to a golden bronze as you temper it with cream that never cheated, but was real cream from its birth, thick, tenderly yellow, perfectly sweet, neither lumpy nor frothing on the Java: such a cup of coffee is a match for twenty blue devils and will exorcise them all."*